G000123875

Discipline Toddlers in a Loving Way

Know What They Understand, How They Develop Mentally, and How to Deal with Bad Behavior

NANCY FOSTER

CONTENTS

Chapter 1	Introduction to Loving Discipline	1
Chapter 2	Understanding and Working with Your Toddler's Psychology... and Why!	7
Chapter 3	Daily Life of your Toddler: Eat, Play, Love (And Don't Forget to Rest!)	32
Chapter 4	Temper Tantrums: Big Feelings Strategy	65
Chapter 5	Punishment: What it Does	85
Chapter 6	Common Issues	100
	About the Autor	107

INTRODUCTION TO LOVING DISCIPLINE

Thanks for choosing Discipline Toddlers in a Loving Way: Know What They Understand, How They Develop Mentally, and How to Deal with Bad Behavior. This book is intended to be used as a guide for any parent or caregiver that wants to learn how to discipline their toddler in a loving and respectful manner.

What is discipline? Culturally, most of us consider discipline to be synonymous with physical punishment, or the inflicting of physical pain or discomfort in order to enforce a behavioral guideline, but this is not necessarily the healthiest or even the most effective way to teach our toddlers how to behave.

Physical punishment places the emphasis on how a parent or caregiver can make the toddler regret their behavior. Loving and respectful discipline emphasizes how a parent or caregiver can guide and teach their toddler the expected and appropriate behavior. Physical punishment often acts as a force that separates parent/caregiver and child, whereas loving and respectful discipline will enforce and maintain the connection between parent/caregiver and child. Children who feel disconnected from their parents and caregivers are more likely to act out, and children who feel more of a safe and secure connection with their parents and caregivers will be more likely to respond positively to correction and modeling.

Loving and respectful discipline does not mean that the parents and caregivers are permissive. Permissive parenting is not loving and respectful, as children look to their parents and caregivers for guidance in how to behave in this world. Boundaries must be set and limits must be held, but they do not need to be attached to a pain-based punishment. Parents and caregivers should allow natural consequences to occur, but creating a means to inflict pain or discomfort on your toddler to "teach" them a lesson is not loving and respectful. In fact, it may be helpful to explore further what message this is sending to our toddlers.

Inflicting pain and discomfort on our toddlers in the name of discipline teaches them that people that are bigger, stronger, and in control have the right to hurt a person that is smaller, weaker, and less capable, in order to "teach a lesson." Our toddlers internalize these messages, and may then go on to do the same with their peers that are smaller, weaker, and less capable than themselves; As adults, we would call this bullying behavior. This is not the message that most parents and caregivers want to send to their toddlers. Ironically, a child that does engage in this form of bullying behavior, would often find themselves further subjected to this behavior from their parents and caregivers in the form of a punishment-based physical discipline tactic such as spanking. This just further reinforces the idea that those that are bigger, stronger, and in control, are allowed to use physical force to inflict pain and discomfort on another person in order to enact their will. This does not teach or guide; It simply reinforces the idea that people use physical force to get what they want.

One idea that may be helpful for parents and caregivers to consider when figuring out what kind of disciplinary techniques they would like to use is to consider what kind of a person they hope their toddler will someday become. Would you like to see your child someday becoming a strong and resourceful leader? Or would you rather like to see your child becoming a passive and obedient follower? If your hope is that your child will someday be a strong and resourceful leader, then you are not likely to help them develop these skills by expecting that they are passively obedient followers as children. Taking into consideration what skills you would like to help your toddler build for their future can help to direct your path towards what disciplinary techniques will work best for you and your family.

Ultimately, toddlers are very "monkey see, monkey do." They do not have to be taught to try to start walking, they will want to walk because they see everyone around them walking. They will pick up a play phone and mimic talking on the phone just as they see the adults in their life talking on phones. Our children are watching us to see how to navigate in this world, and by modeling appropriate behaviors, we can guide and teach the behaviors we want to see rather than attempt to physically punish them into regretting the behaviors we do not want to see.

Decide what values and character traits are most important to you, and make a conscious effort to model those to your toddler in everything you do. This book will help you to better understand your child's psychology and how they think and mentally develop so you can help them to be their very best. You will learn how loving and respectful discipline can be used throughout their early years, starting as newborns, and how the various stages of development reflect their capabilities.

Understanding your child's psychological and developmental capabilities will help you to better understand how to assist them in the work of their daily life, including eating, sleeping, playing, and loving. Their little brains are still developing, and areas that are directly responsible for self-control are just not developed enough for us to expect them to succeed under those expectations. Our toddlers are growing up in a tech-heavy world, and learning how this affects them developmentally and how we can better support tech use in a healthy manner will be helpful in learning how to appropriately and respectfully teach and guide them.

You will learn how to better understand, prevent, and deal with toddler tantrums. There are many parts of successfully dealing with our toddler's big feelings, and you will learn several strategies for success. Some of these strategies for success may even be surprising to you, but just as every toddler is different, so is every parent and caregiver, and so what may work best for you and your child may not work best for another. This book will explain how to do this and will encourage you to try various strategies for success so you can figure out what is the best fit for your family.

There has been a significant amount of striking research that has been released over the last several years about punitive physical punishment and its negative side-effects. This book will discuss some of the punishment pitfalls and how to avoid them, as well as how to alleviate any negative side-effects that have already been incurred from prior punitive punishment. It is never too late for us to change course and try something new. When we know better, we do better.

Lastly, this book will discuss some common issues that parents and caregivers of toddlers face in their daily discipline routines. All too often, we view toddlers as being a separate class of people, in need of severe and swift correction so they can behave the way we want them to, which unfortunately often runs counter to what they are developmentally capable of. Toddlers are worthy of our loving and respectful guidance, and reading this book as a parent/caregiver is a great first step towards that end.

UNDERSTANDING AND WORKING WITH YOUR TODDLER'S PSYCHOLOGY... AND WHY!

There is a reason why it has become culturally accepted to view our tiny toddlers as almost an entirely different class of people, and sometimes even as an entirely different species! This is tongue in cheek, of course, but there are many reasons for why it can be so difficult for parents and caregivers to understand their tiny toddler's behavior, especially at the stage commonly referred to as the Terrible Twos! Babies come into this world entirely dependent on their parents and caregivers, and we are physically able to control most aspects of their lives in those very early days. As our babies become more mobile, this becomes more and more difficult to do, and once the toddler years hit, this newfound mobility is tied to a cognitive leap that inspires our little one's to assert this newfound independence in ways that can be very trying for the adults around them!

Infant Guidance

To better understand how loving and respectful discipline works for our toddlers, let's first look at the role of loving and respectful discipline that begins as soon as our babies enter into this world. As we touched on in the introduction, discipline does not equal punishment. When we refer to discipline for newborns, we are certainly not referring to or condoning any sort of physical punishment that uses pain or discomfort to enforce a behavioral guideline. We are instead referring to discipline in its positive association, as a tool to teach and guide. While the newborn stage may not seem like the age that we are doing much beyond around the clock direct care (feeding, changing diapers, bathing, etc.) our responsive care and attention is teaching and guiding our little ones towards an important lesson. We are teaching them that they can count on us, and we are there for them. Discipline can be and is as simple as that.

In that first year of life, our tiny, precious babies are learning what to expect of the world and what relationships look like. What they learn from their parents and caregivers in these very early days will set the stage for the development of their sense of self and their self-esteem as they continue to develop. When we are responsive to our baby's cries and physical cues and meet their needs efficiently, lovingly, and respectfully, we are teaching them that they are cared for, supported, and worthy of attention and love. These are considered to be the fundamental building blocks of a healthy sense of self and self-esteem.

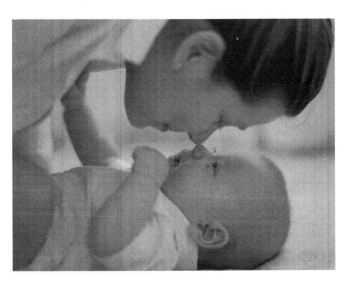

It can be a common fear of some parents and caregivers they might "spoil" their baby by meeting their every cry and their every cue, but the American Academy of Pediatrics- the United State's foremost authority on child health and development- states that this is simply not the case. You have a baby, not a perishable food item- there is no such thing as a spoiled baby! They even go on to assert that research shows that the more responsive we are to these very early needs in infancy, the less likely our little ones are to need extra reassurance as they enter the toddler years. This early foundation of trust is very important to our future toddler's mental, emotional, and psychological health.

Leaps and Bounds

The one-year mark is what is widely considered to be when your child hits the toddler years. There is so much happening in our little one's world at this age, isn't there? Most children are taking their first steps around this time, and their vocabulary is growing in leaps and bounds. Some days it may even seem like our little one is growing and learning in their sleep, as they often seem to master new skills and abilities almost overnight. Their brains are like little sponges in these early toddler days, and they keep parents and caregivers on their toes with their curiosity and newfound independence. While it is impressive to see our little ones as they grow and develop so quickly, there is somewhat of a drawback to this. These huge leaps may lead us to believe that our little ones are capable of more than they may actually be capable of, developmentally.

This is where understanding our toddler's psychology comes into play. There are so many developmental leaps that our toddlers are making in the years between ages 1-3. Just imagine what must be taking place under the surface as our toddler goes from taking their first halting and unsteady steps as a wobbly one-year-old to when they are scaling playground equipment by themselves to go down the slide at the neighborhood park just a few short months later!

These toddler transformations are exactly the sorts of significant physical leaps and milestones that are prevalent in the toddler years, including the easily visible ones such as learning to use their bodies to walk, run, and jump.

Fine motor skills, such as the ability to pick up tiny objects such as pebbles or Lego pieces are developing. These are the skills that toddlers will need to be able to do everyday tasks such as brushing their teeth, buttoning up their jacket, holding silverware properly, holding and using a pencil, etc. They are any movement that requires use and coordination of the small muscles in the hands.

Gross motor skills, such as the ability to throw a ball, are developing. Their little bodies must learn how to do everything in these early years: they must learn how to climb stairs, how to open doors, how to dress themselves. Gross motor skills are the skills that involve movement of the whole body and require a core strength, such as when balancing on one foot while putting the other into a shoe. Both strength and coordination are developing quickly in these early toddler years.

Toddlers are developing quickly on the cognitive level, too. Their ability to learn and partake in social customs, such as waving hello and goodbye, saying "sorry," when they've done something wrong, and to begin to learn their colors, numbers, letters, nursery rhymes, etc. is all taking place at break-neck speed, especially if we were to compare it to the rates of learning that most adults are typically working at!

Social and emotional skills are the skills that our

toddlers need to be able to successfully navigate social situations such as school, work and life. These are the skills that will help our children develop their friendships, manage conflict resolution, manage and handle stress, learn how to make sound decisions and use good judgement, and to develop empathy skills. Parents and caregivers provide the primary model here for these skills, and just as our responsive care in infancy helps to set the foundation for a strong and healthy sense of self and self-esteem, parents and caregivers must also model the social and emotional skills that we want our toddlers to have.

It is unrealistic for parents and caregivers to expect for a two-year-old child to control and manage their own emotions without having a temper tantrum if they watch their parents and their caregivers act out in emotional distress by yelling and slamming doors. Again, our sweet little toddlers are very monkey see, monkey do. Developing emotional regulation is a long process for most toddlers.

Respectful Expectation

As our toddlers are experiencing this expedited rate of physical, developmental, cognitive, social, and emotional growth, it is only natural that some of this may be unsettling for both them and their parents and caregivers. From their limited perspective, the world is so wide and so wondrous.

It is also full of so many intriguing things to do, see, and touch, and they often spend most of their days hearing the word "no" as they reach out to explore! From their viewpoint, they only know that the dog's bowl of water on the floor is wet, and they remember that they enjoy exploring wet things and are encouraged to explore water in the bathtub or in the kiddie pool in the backyard, so why not this convenient water source right here in the house? Yet, perplexingly, every time they go near it, they hear "no!" and are moved away from it.

Or perhaps they find themselves watching their parents and caregivers spend their days touching, looking at, and interacting with this portable object that they carry around with them from room to room and place to place, but when their little toddler hands reach out to touch it, they are told "no!" when all they want to do is explore this intriguing object just as they see their primary models do. They don't understand that the smart phone has been placed on the charger and needs to be left alone. All the toddler knows is that this thing that gets a lot of attention and use from everyone else is now finally within their reach, and they'd like to check it out too!

This leads us to one of the major aspects that parents and caregivers must understand about toddlers and their psychology. They are learning how to be and who to be in this world, primarily from looking to see what others do. As parents and caregivers, it can be easy to become preoccupied with ensuring we say the right things to our children, and impart the right wisdom to them at different parts of their lives, but this is not how toddlers learn best. Toddlers will not learn that they should not play in the dog's water bowl after hearing a lengthy explanation about how that is the dog's drinking water, and that splashing in it will make a mess that will then need to be cleaned up. Toddler's will not understand that the phone must be left alone to charge and is not for them after hearing their parents/caregiver's long lecture to leave it alone because otherwise the phone will die and then some important communication may be missed. We need to better recognize where our toddlers are coming from, because our toddlers are not operating from a place where they have the cognitive understanding and the impulse control necessary to understand and act accordingly. In this, it is up to us to structure our world to better accommodate them where they are at.

Toddlers' brains are still in the development phase and it is simply unrealistic to expect our toddlers to be able to fulfill certain behavioral expectations that they are not yet equipped with the proper tools yet to do so. We are referring here specifically to the pre-frontal cortex, which is that part of the brain that is responsible for impulse control and the ability to make sound decisions and control our emotions. Once we recognize that our toddlers are simply not fully equipped with the tools required to meet these expectations, we can then make the shift away from these unrealistic expectations that only cause parents, caregivers, and the toddlers themselves strife. Consider this: Our toddlers do not want to be in the position of making their parents and caregivers unhappy with them, but it can often be that it is our expectations that play a large role in setting them up for this failure of sorts.

It can also be helpful to recognize that the only means our toddlers have to explore and learn about the world around them is through direct manipulation and experimentation, and this is hands on. Their learning is tactile. They have to use their hands to touch and their eyes to inspect. They have to use their nose to smell and yes, even their mouth to taste! (All toddler parents and caregivers are unfortunately all too well acquainted with that particular mode of exploration!) This hands-on experimentation is the only way our toddlers can access and learn about their worlds. If we think about it for a moment, they are not able to pick up their smart phones and do a quick internet search to learn about something that interests them, or run to their local library and ask a librarian for help in finding information on a topic. Picking up an object and giving it a quick taste may be the best they can do with certain things!

What's more, is that our toddlers are in a position of having to learn everything from the bottom up. They are new in this world, and it is big, confusing, and full of people telling them what to do and how to do it. Take a brief moment to truly consider what it is like for a toddler child: They are put down to sleep when they may not actually be sleepy yet, in a bed that has bars and is set up specifically to contain them and keep them in. If they wake in the middle of the night, there is no ability to reach for a drink of water or go grab a late-night snack by themselves, they must cry and yell until someone else comes to their aid. Then once morning arrives, they are still stuck in their bed and must do the same, yelling and crying until someone comes to them. Even once they are pulled out of their crib, their day has been planned for them. They are dressed in clothes they didn't pick out, they are subjected to hygiene rituals they can't do and likely don't completely understand the reason for them, they are fed foods they didn't choose and prepare, and then they are placed in situations they didn't choose, either strapped in a car seat and taken somewhere or set down in a room full of interesting objects such as electronic cords or curtains that they are then told "no!" about when they try to explore them. Their days continue on like this, very little freedom and autonomy and a "no" at every turn. Can you imagine how frustrating this must be for them, especially as they are going through so many developmental leaps and learning and developing new skills and abilities every day?

Parents and caregivers must first evaluate their

expectations as the first step. Are they expecting something that is beyond their toddler's ability level? Think back to the example of the water dish on the floor. Evaluating this scenario against the knowledge that not only are toddlers essentially hard-wired to learn about the world around them by directly exploring, but that part of their brain that is necessary for them to check this desire to explore against the ongoing direction of "no" is not even fully developed yet. It is necessary to adjust expectations.

Rather than expect that a toddler will be able to curb their self-impulses and desire to explore the dog's water dish, recognize that this is a monumental task for them that borders on the impossible, and instead, remove the toddler's access to the dog's water dish.

We spoke earlier about all of the "no" that our toddlers hear day in, and day out, as they seek to explore and learn about the world in the only way they know how. All of these "no's" contribute to a feeling of frustration and irritation for both the parents, caregivers, and toddlers. A way to easily alleviate this frustration and irritation is to avoid it in the first place. An easy way to do this is to give your toddler the opposite of "no." Give them a space that is only "yes," where they are allowed to touch and explore everything in it. For some people, this space may be a gated off room full of toys, manipulatives, and anything that is toddler safe and friendly, and for others this may just be a toddler playpen area in a living room that is full of toys, manipulatives, and anything that is toddler safe and friendly. It should go without saying that any space that is devoted to yes will need to be as childproofed as possible, because the entire point is to give them a space where they can safely play and explore without hearing the dreaded "no." This means no bookcases that can be climbed on and pulled over, no end tables with a lamp on it that can be pulled down, no houseplants on a side table that could be knocked over, nothing at all that the toddler will be told "no" about if they pick it up.

This opposite of the "no" space gives both toddlers and their parents and caregivers relief and freedom. Just as much as a toddler grows tired and frustrated of being thwarted with that dastardly "no," parents and caregivers can quickly tire of having to chase after the curious and explorative toddler and redirect and manage them time and time again. This safe space that gives the toddler freedom and space to explore, learn, and play is called the "yes space" by RIE philosophy proponents. RIE philosophy is a infant/child philosophy that emphasizes respect in parent/caregiver relationships with infants, toddlers, and beyond. This "yes space" is very important in building this respectful relationship, as just as badly as our toddlers want to explore and learn about their world, they also want to do well. They don't want to be chastised and lectured to repeatedly, they want to succeed! Setting up a "yes space" is an important part of setting our toddlers up for success.

Setting up safe spaces for toddlers in the home is important, but what about when we need to take them out with us? If a parent or caregiver needs to run errands, such as heading to the grocery store and then swinging by the post office, what should they expect their toddler to be capable of behaviorally and psychologically? Well, it can be helpful to first consider that for most of us adults, trips to the grocery store and the post office aren't necessarily what we consider to be the definition of a "good time," so perhaps its not so very different for our toddler- except they will have very little tasks to do on these trips and will instead only be along for the ride!

There are essentially two basic schools of thought on taking our toddlers along with us to run errands. One says that it is healthy for our toddlers to accompany their parents and caregivers on tasks such as visits to the grocery store and post office, so they can have the opportunity to learn and practice appropriate behavior in these spaces. The other says that it is disrespectful to our toddlers and unrealistic for parents and caregivers to expect that toddler's will be able to meet our expectations on errands such as these.

Both of these schools of thought are operating on the model of wanting to set our toddlers up for success, aren't they? For the first, the idea is sound that our toddlers will never learn how to behave in these sorts of scenarios if they aren't given opportunities to learn and practice meeting our expectations. Their primary mode of learning comes from observation of their parents and caregivers as they navigate through the world, and so how will a toddler come to learn appropriate behavior in the grocery store or standing in line at the post office, if they never get to see what that looks like?

For many parents and caregivers, this is not even a choice they are able to make, as it is simply necessity to take their toddler along with them to run errands. A way to set up the trip for success is to begin by adjusting our expectations. A two-year-old is not going to find it easy to stand in a long line, creeping at a snail's pace, at the post office. There are things that parents and caregivers can do to help, such as bringing a small toy and/or snack for the toddler to engage with after the excitement of the new place they are in has faded, and to recognize and realize that in a scenario such as a post office, there may be some physical restraint needed to keep their toddler from running around the room. Some parents and caregivers opt to use carriers that allow them to strap their toddler on their front or back, or strollers, so they can be safely restrained and the parent and/or caregiver can still take care of what they came to take care of. Most toddlers enjoy these options greatly as it gives them a safe and secure location to observe and take in their new surroundings, and it gives them the structure and boundary that they need to keep from running around and getting in trouble. Again, we have to remember as parents and caregivers that our toddlers want to succeed, too!

For parents and caregivers that opt not to take their toddlers along on errands that involve putting them in scenarios in which they will not be likely to succeed, the idea there is that it is more respectful of the toddler's needs and developmental level and also the parents, caregivers, and everyone else at the grocery store and/or post office to not introduce their toddler into a situation that they will likely not do well in. No one enjoys having to navigate and deal with a toddler temper tantrum in the dairy aisle!

There is no one right answer here, only what works best for you and your family. Some toddlers are very easy-going and amenable to days out spent running errand after errand. Other toddlers may be more resistant to days spent getting in and out of the car and going into place after place that requires them to engage in very non-toddler like behavior, such as being quiet and sitting still! Just as with most things parenting, every family is different and must find what works best for them. The most important aspect to keep in mind here, as with many things related to loving discipline, is checking in with ourselves to see if we are guiding our toddlers positively and respectfully.

Building Relationships

Parent-child relationships are very important to toddler development. It is the first model of relationships that most children have, so how we are with our tiny toddlers will set the foundation for how our toddlers will interact in relationships with others throughout their lives.

Secure attachment, or the positive relationship that a child has with their parents/caregivers that they know they can depend on their parents/caregivers for physical and emotional support and safety. The presence of this type of relationship plays a strong role in a child's sense of safety and independence.

As toddlers learn how to build relationships based on their relationships in these early, formative years, there is a piece of the puzzle that is sometimes lost: that of the father figure. Families can be constructed in many different forms, including families that have a mother and a grandmother as the two primary caregivers, families that have a single mother as the primary caregiver, families that have two mothers as the primary caregiver, and many, many more combinations. It is not that there must be the person that shares DNA present in our toddler's life, but there needs to be a person that is able to model what a healthy and successful male relationship looks like (just as it is important to have a person that is able to model what a healthy and successful female relationship looks like). If the biological father is not present, and there is no stepfather, or close uncle or grandfather available to help model this healthy and successful male relationship, then a family can seek out other ways to be sure this relationship is modeled, such as with a close family friend.

The importance here is in recognizing that for young girls, their relationship with a father figure is a model for their future relationships with males and what sort of treatment and relationship they will seek out and tolerate. For young boys, their relationships with a father figure is a model for their future selves, as they often model themselves after this primary male influence. Without a strong father figure, young boys will often model themselves after the nearest available male, which may or may not be the sort of influence that parents and caregivers want their young boys to be influenced by.

Becoming more aware of how we are structuring our toddler's lives, from their environment to the people in it, is an important part of disciplining toddlers in a loving way. Understanding their psychology and how we can better relate to them respectfully goes a long way to ensuring we are creating a loving environment that contributes to parents and caregivers abilities to guide and teach our toddlers well.

Useful Information and Tips for This Chapter

Development phases of the baby

Clinical and developmental psychologists examine this process through the developmental stages through which the child passes in the earliest period:

0-2 months: the child is primarily directed at himself, and in interaction with the environment reacts almost to each person

2-6 months: the child responds directly to family members

6-8 months: strong attachment to the mother, shows clear signs of fear when the mother is not nearby

8-12 months: the child slowly emerges from the symbiotic relationship with the mother, it is important that the mother reacts to the child's independent movements in order not to prevent the separation and individuation of the child that begins at this stage. The child shows separation fears due to emotional separation from the mother and uses "transient objects" (stuffed toys, blankets)

Intellectual development

The intellectual development of a child in the first year takes place through the training of senses and movements. Thus, in the first six weeks, the baby is practicing reflex movements, in order to be able to manage them in the second month. During the third and fourth month, the child repeats actions aimed at exploring one's own body (for example, repeating the same movement by a hand or foot), and from the fourth to the ninth month will repeat acts directed to the external environment (throwing the toy in the same way).

Until the baby turns six months, if the parents pull the toy from her sight, she does not look for it. But at an average age of six months, the baby starts looking for an object that is out of her sight, which means she begins to understand that the objects exist independently of her field of vision.

Incentive of development

From seven to eight months, the child can distinguish the means from the objective and anticipate events, so for example if he cries and mom or dad enters the room, the child ceases to cry because he predicts comforting. When a child begins to crawl, parents can, in a simple way, through the game, encourage him to solve the problem, they can put an obstacle (a larger toy or pillow) between the child and the toy the child is headed to. The child will crawl up to the obstacle, remove it, and reach the desired target. Because of this, the hiding games that children also like at a later age are encouraging the intellectual development of children in a certain way, because they teach that objects exist independently of them and that they can solve the problem and reach the goal.

The emotional and intellectual development of the child is complex and inseparable from the overall physical progress, so all of the mentioned ages are averages, and subject to individual variations. It is only important that parents, in the course of monitoring the development of the child, be directed to induce and encourage their development.

10 Things That Make the Baby Happy

Observing your child and appreciating what makes him happy is one of the ways to strengthen a relationship with a child. These are some of the things that babies love most:

1. Babies like when they are naked

For some babies is enough just to remove their clothes and diaper to calm down. There is a constant connection between the body and the feelings of the baby, and since they can not speak, their body expresses all their feelings. For this reason, babies want to get rid of all tensions and be as free as they can in their bodies. When they are naked, babies seem to receive and express their emotions more easily. They differently see the world around themselves when they are without clothes and it is easier for them to explore and get to know their environment.

2. The babies like to be cuddled

It reminds them of the time spent in the womb, in the stomach of their mother, when they were surrounded by "walls" that protected them and provided shelter. In the first few weeks of life, many babies feel satisfied when their mothers wrap them into the blanket and carry them; they like the sense of intimacy. Gradually, babies feel freer and start making the first safer and more confident movements.

3. Touching your mother's skin

Mother's embrace is the best solution for almost all problems. Many studies have shown that direct contact with the body, more precisely with the skin, between mother and baby, balances the baby's body temperature and heart rate, and helps the secretion of endorphins and oxytocin hormones, the hormone of love, not only in the baby but also in the mother. In contact with the mother's skin, the nerve system of the newborn relaxes and thus improves the relationship between mother and child, since both feel close and loved.

4. Monotone sounds

Monotone sounds (sound of the motor, washing machine ...) resembles the sounds that baby has been listening for 9 months in the mother's stomach, and it relaxes them. These sounds that reach the baby are mostly muted, as well as the sounds in the stomach.

5. Music

Music is a stimulus for learning: its high and low tones stimulate neural connections, reorganize the brain and, depending on the type of music (classical, modern ...), help the baby in different ways. Harmonic sounds dominated by high tones are preparing a baby for learning. Low tone melodies relax the baby. The baby feels the voices of her parents as music: higher tones are mommy's and lower daddy's.

6. Mom's scent

Many babies who have trouble sleeping relax when mom put a piece of her clothes into the crib. The first thing newborn feels with his senses is parents smell. The sense of smell is associated with the urge to survive, and for newborns, it is crucial to recognize and remember the smell of their parents after birth; without it, it is helpless. Although they do not see well, newborns can recognize their parents by smell. The mother's arms are one of the happiest places for the baby - she feels the smell of her mother and knows she is safe.

7. Walks

Many kids require more attention and are crying more when they are at home than when they are outdoors. Babies feel that air is not the same inside and outside the house; they notice the difference between the air in motion and stagnant air from indoors. Apart from the air, the sounds and smells differ from the outside. Senses of hearing and smell are very developed since birth, for this reason a walk around the park is the best way for a baby to relax by feeling new smells and listening to new sounds - all this develops an adventurous spirit in the baby!

8. Babies like to stick everything in their mouths

The mouth is the baby's "third eye": they help the baby to meet the world that surrounds her. When a baby is sucking various objects, she reveals their taste, texture, density, weight ... She gets information that she could not get only by observing the object. During the first two years of life, a baby's mouth is a kind of scanner that helps them create an image in their brain of what is out there.

9. Rocking

Rocking consists of uniform, rhythmic movements that connect the baby with their senses with safety and balance. On the one hand, rocking develops deeper neural connections, and on the other hand, monotonous and predictable rhythms are associated with the stability of the child. The baby gets the security and confidence in her mother, and the more familiar her rhythm is, the more relaxed she is, she releases more endorphins and more quickly adapt to the environment.

10. Mommy's voice

Mother's voice is one of the things that contain everything that makes the baby feel peaceful: it contains music, high tones that stimulate learning, and most importantly - the desire to communicate with the baby. Every time a mother turns to the baby, the baby registers a number of emotions, which awake her desire to learn to speak. As soon as they become capable of it, the babies answer you with giggly. Communicating with parents is their greatest wish.

DAILY LIFE OF YOUR TODDLER: EAT, PLAY, LOVE (AND DON'T FORGET TO REST!)

There is no doubt about it, the toddler years are a time of immense learning, growing, and development. There are so many things that our toddlers are learning daily, and parents and caregivers are responsible for providing the structure and the tools for success as our toddlers explore their worlds and learn how to make sense of each day as it comes.

Parents and caregivers of toddlers know that each day is ripe with opportunities to guide and teach our little ones how to be successful in their daily tasks, such as eating, playing, relating to others, and sleeping. Loving and respectful discipline includes the guidance and structure that gives toddlers the tools they need to be successful in these areas.

Eating Habits

If we were to take a poll of toddler parents and enquire into their daily eating habits, it would be expected that there would be many that would lament their toddler's appetite fluctuations or their pickiness and preferences, or perhaps their table manners. This is all too common, particularly in Western culture. There are some cultural reasons for this. In Western culture, it is common for toddlers to be served food throughout the day, in small snacking amounts, but then to also be expected to sit through the standard family meals three times a day, even when they are not all that hungry and when they have not been expected to sit still for that length of time and eat that much in that sort of setting. It is also common for toddlers to often be given the bland, tasteless, and soft textured foods marketed towards them, rather than allowing them to explore and learn a variety of tastes and textures. There is also often a certain element of pressure and power struggle that accompanies meal times with toddlers that creates more struggle and negative associations around meal times than is necessary or helpful.

To begin, it can be helpful to reframe how we feel about our toddler's eating habits into a loving and respectful discipline mindset. These early toddler years are an excellent time for parents and caregivers to facilitate a healthy relationship between their toddlers and food. Power struggles and pressure only serve to create angst and anxiety around eating and food choices, and contribute to picky and resistant future eaters as well.

A healthy relationship with food is one in which food is being used for nourishment and health, and not for comfort and appeasement of others. If we set up a dynamic in which our toddlers are being forced to eat a certain amount of food to appease us and meet an arbitrary guideline, then we are teaching them that their relationship to food is externally driven, rather than an intuitive practice in which they take in food for their nourishment and health.

This is one of the spots that can become particularly tricky for parents and caregivers. To begin with, we all know that our toddlers *must* eat! How is it then, that there are days where our toddlers seem quite content to exist on a handful of cheerios and nothing more? This is completely normal. Toddler appetites can fluctuate wildly, both from day to day and even meal to meal. This is due in large part because their little bodies are going through growth spurts, or periods of expedited growth, that can require a boost in calorie intake, and then once the growth spurt has ended, they go back to their previous calorie requirements. There is also the daily distraction of a new and shiny world that they are desperate to explore that can also make it easy for them to prioritize playing over sitting down to eat a full meal.

There is a healthy eating model called the division of responsibility in feeding that is recommended by several leading health agencies, including The Academy of Nutrition and Dietetics, The American Academy of Pediatrics, the Expert Committee on Child Obesity, Head Start, the WIC program, and the USDA Food and Nutrition Service. The division of responsibility in feeding model, or the DOR, was developed by Ellen Satter, who was a family therapist, nutritionist, and dietician. Her model for how to encourage and guide children towards a healthy relationship with food has been proven successful time and time again.

The ultimate goal of DOR model is to encourage what the Ellen Satter Institute refers to as eating competency. This is the healthy relationship in food that was mentioned earlier. With that goal in mind, DOR lays out guidelines for parents and caregivers to follow when feeding children, beginning in infancy.

The DOR guideline is that parents and caregivers are responsible for what toddlers are offered to eat, when toddlers are offered food, and where toddlers will be fed, and toddlers are responsible for how much and whether or not they will eat any of the foods that have been offered to them. This may be surprising to some, but the basic tenet here is that parents and caregivers are tasked with being sure that a variety of nutritious and healthy foods are available to their children, and they must trust that their children will know how much food they need to eat. It does require trust that our toddlers will not starve themselves, and it also requires structuring meal times in such a way that allows toddlers to be active participants rather than passive bystanders that are experiencing feeding as something being done to them.

There are many ways to encourage the active participation of toddlers during mealtimes and their autonomy and responsibility in feeding themselves. One way is to ensure that there is always at least one item on their plate that parents and caregivers know that the toddler will eat. Perhaps your toddler is on an apple kick, and has yet to turn down an apple slice. While offering a lunchtime plate that includes slices of rotisserie chicken and cubes of white cheddar cheese that sometimes your toddler likes and sometimes your toddler doesn't, be sure to include a few slices of apple so that there is always something there that you know your toddler will eat. This is setting both parents, caregivers, and toddlers up for success.

As was mentioned above in the toddler psychology section, toddlers do not want to be at odds with their parents and caregivers. They do not want to be in a position in which they are displeasing parents and caregivers and getting in trouble. They also do not want to be pressured to eat something they do not like or are not in the mood for. This is no different than an adult that does not feel very hungry for lunch one day and decides to opt for a granola bar on the go vs a full, sit down meal. The idea here is to allow our toddlers to develop their own internal, intuitive sense of what their body needs; this is a significant part of a healthy relationship with food. For instance, how many adults were forced to finish everything on their plate before leaving the dinner table as children, even if their stomachs were full or they did not like what they were eating enough to continue eating it? What was the takeaway here? Beyond the economic aspect of not wanting to waste any bit of food, the message to the mind and the body is that eating is not something that is done for nourishment, but rather a mindless task that must be completed until an arbitrary amount has been consumed, regardless of what the body wants. This is not a healthy relationship with food, and it is reflected in our culture with many experiencing conflicted values with food such as binge-eating, comfort eating, food and calorie restriction, etc.

There are some additional methods for setting parents, caregivers, and toddlers up for success at mealtimes. Let your toddler be involved in the experience as much as possible. Perhaps you can ask your toddler what color cup they would like their water in? What color napkin? What color plate? You can ask your toddler to set the table with their napkin and utensils. You can offer choices such as, "would you like to have 3 or 4 apple slices? Would you like yellow cheese or white cheese?" Be aware that there is a catch here. If you are asking your toddler to make these choices, then any of their choices must be okay and honored. Do not offer a choice between cheeses if you are not able to or don't want to honor it. Do not offer the red cup or the green cup if the red cup is in the dishwasher, etc.

When parents and caregivers allow their toddlers to make choices around their experiences, they give them a sense of ownership and autonomy over the experience, and this contributes to a toddler's feeling of involvement and their desire to be a part of the mealtime experience. Another way to do this is to allow your toddler to eat as they would like to eat. Offer proper utensils, be sure your toddler knows how to use them if they would like to, and model how you are using them, but allow your toddler to use their fingers to pick up their avocado cubes rather than their fork. Allow your toddler to further develop those fine motor skills by picking up each individual spaghetti noodle to eat, one at a time, if that's what they want to do. Understand that mealtime is still a part of their learning and exploration! They are learning colors, textures, tastes. So many of the negative feelings and associations that parents, caregivers, and toddlers have around food and mealtimes are attached to this experience of control. Again, parents and caregivers control the what, the when, and the where of feeding, but toddlers have ultimate control over how much they will eat and even if they will eat any of it at all. This is an important part of using loving and respectful guidance in helping to shape our toddler's healthy relationship with food.

Another area that contributes to facilitating your toddler's healthy relationship with food is in providing an environment for eating that is relaxed, peaceful, and social. Family meals should take place at a table where conversation can be had and the meal can be enjoyed and savored together. This small step cannot be taken lightly, because there is a significant difference in how long a toddler will be able to sit at a table surrounded by family that is talking and interacting with one another vs how long a toddler will be able to sit by themselves with a plate of food. The former is demonstrating that mealtimes are comfortable and enjoyable. The latter is demonstrating that mealtimes are a solitary event to be gotten through to get to something more interesting. There is also need for recognizing that even at a table full of family that is laughing and enjoying one another, a toddler's ability to sit still at this table for long lengths of time is simply not present for most. Releasing that expectation and instead recognizing that once your toddler has stopped eating their food and is now trying to get down, they are letting you know that that is all they could handle of sitting still. All toddler behavior is communication, and this is what a squirmy, wiggly, toddler at the dinner table is telling their parents and caregivers.

Playtime

Playtime! For most adults, it is easy to associate playtime as time spent goofing off or maybe even as a waste of time, but for toddlers, it is so much more. Maria Montessori, the founder and creator of the Montessori system of schooling, famously stated that "Play is the work of the child," and this could not be more true. What may look like a waste of time to an adult, is a toddler whose brain is rapidly developing and making new connections as they explore, handle, and manipulate the world around them. Play is where toddlers will learn how to interact with their world and everything in it. The wooden puzzle pieces they are working with offer an opportunity to develop their cognitive and problem-solving skills, to better develop their fine motor skills and their hand and eye coordination, and to experience the feeling of pride that helps to build their self-esteem when they finally are able to place each piece in its proper place. The building block set they are using gives toddlers the opportunity to practice their fine and gross motor skills, to develop their hand and eye coordination, use their imagination and then be able to physically manipulate it into reality, and to build their engineering skills as they learn to recognize what works when building a tower and what doesn't. Shape sorters that require toddlers to place the appropriate shape through the appropriate slot encourage problem solving, spatial awareness, and perseverance, as they learn by the repetitive try-fail-try-fail-try-win model. Dolls and other figurines provide tools for toddlers to engage in the imaginative play that helps them explore and reinforce what they are learning about social dynamics and interactions. A wooden spoon and a plastic mixing bowl turned upside down are a drumstick and drum set that can be used to explore sound, rhythm, and beat. Toys do not need to be fancy or store-bought. They simply need to be accessible and safe.

According to the Montessori model, play is responsible for allowing children to grow socially, build their creativity muscles, and expand and strengthen their problem-solving skills, language skills, and physical skills. The Montessori model encourages open-ended toys that may be used and manipulated by children in a variety of ways, and that encourage children to use their imagination to solve problems, cooperate with others, and engage their creativity. An example of open-ended toys would be toys like Legos and blocks that a toddler can choose what they want to do with rather than a game set with a specific set of rules that must be followed in order to engage with the game.

Toddlers often make the leap from solitary play to parallel play around the age of two. Solitary play is what babies typically do, where they can fixate on an object of interest alone and by themselves for large periods of time, without needing anyone else to interact with or engage with them. Toddlers and children much older will still engage in solitary play, but toddlers make the shift to parallel play, which is where they will play alongside their peers, but not in a way that appears that they are necessarily interacting together. They may be playing with similar toys or completely different toys, but they are playing side by side and enjoying the company of another child nearby. Group play doesn't typically develop until around the age of three. Then children are ready to being playing cooperatively and interactively, sharing and taking turns. Before then, toddlers may appear to be uninterested in playing "together," but parallel play side by side still offers social advantages for them at that time. All of these forms of play are useful and healthy and toddlers should always be allowed to pursue the form of play they are authentically drawn to at the time without being pushed into another by parents and caregivers.

As each of these forms of play have their place, the most important aspect in each is that children should be allowed to develop their own play themes. Toddlers do not need their parents and caregivers to tell or show them how to play. They simply need to be provided with a safe and accessible space to explore safe and interesting toys. In fact, this is a part of the loving and respectful guidance that allows them autonomy and choice in a safe situation.

Loving our Toddlers with a Routine

Toddlers are growing and developing so quickly, and every day is full of new discoveries! While this is incredibly exciting for parents and caregivers to witness, there are times that this may be overwhelming for our precious toddlers who are going through it. An important aspect in providing a loving and respectful guidance for our toddlers during this time of great change and excitement, is to provide a constant routine.

Routine can sadly sometimes be associated with a negative perception of staleness, sameness, or a boring life. This could not be further from the truth for toddlers! For toddlers, routine provides a sense of safety and predictability, where they are able to understand and prepare for the next step in their day to day lives. As we discussed above, toddlers do not have much freedom and autonomy in their daily lives, but having a set routine allows our toddlers to know what to expect during their days. If every day, the routine is brush teeth, read book, then lay down for bed, then the surprise of bedtime is removed every evening because your toddler is able to anticipate each next step and feel the sense of security of knowing that there is a comforting predictability and a sense of sureness to their days.

There is also an ease of mind that comes with knowing what to expect that is all too often unavailable to toddlers. They go through their days being surprised and perplexed by the world around them, surely it must be comforting for them to know what to expect every night after they brush their teeth, right?

According to Aha! Parenting magazine, there are several benefits to implementing routines. One is that it decreases power struggles because the toddler is able to understand what is coming next rather than being taken by surprise by what their parent/caregiver is expecting of them. This also increases cooperation and encourages our toddlers to actively participate; for example, if there is always a bedtime story after brushing teeth, then not only will our toddler be a willing participant in the teeth brushing to get to their story quicker, but they may even go to their bookshelf and pick the book they want to read without being prompted! Following a routine also allows for toddlers to learn how to look ahead; for example, if you are going to the park "after lunch," then your toddler knows that "lunch" is the event that will come before the park. They can't look at the clock to know when noon is, but they understand that lunch will be served, they will eat, and then they will go the park. This allows for a smoother transition for all.

It has also been observed that toddlers whose lives follow a predictable daily routine are more independent and engaged in their environment. When parents and caregivers provide toddlers with a daily routine, toddlers feel secure in what their days will look like, and are more comfortable in reaching out to engage in their environment. This does not mean that there can never be breaks in the routine or surprises, it just means that when these do come, our toddlers are already in a steady, secure, and comfortable place and are better equipped to deal with the unexpected.

Routine and Rest

With great routine, comes great rest! As with the rest of their days, toddlers thrive on a predictable sleep schedule. To begin, let's look at some of the toddler sleep guidelines that have been given by the American Academy of Sleep Medicine that have been endorsed by the American Academy of Pediatrics. The American Academy of Sleep Medicine recommends that children between one and two years old should sleep between eleven and fourteen hours per day (including their naps) and that children between three and five should sleep between ten to thirteen hours per day (including their naps). The American Academy of Sleep Medicine also gives several advantages to ensuring that our children get an adequate amount of daily sleep, including improved behavior, learning, memory, attention, emotional regulation, and mental and physical health! That's more than enough to inspire parents and caregivers to ensure their toddlers are getting enough sleep, isn't it?

Now the question remains, how? Most parents and caregivers have experienced one or two hiccups related to sleep and their toddler, often including falling asleep and then staying asleep. It may be helpful to first ensure that parents and caregivers are viewing the process as a facilitator of helping their toddlers to get the kind of restorative and restful sleep that is so crucial during this period of intense growth and development, and also as a guide for future healthy sleep habits. This is a part of creating a firm foundation for the rest of their lives. Just as with so many of the other areas that parents and caregivers are tasked with guiding and teaching toddlers to be successful in, restful sleep is something that toddlers often blossom with the right mindset from the people they look to for guidance. This is an area that all too often results in struggle, as parents and caregivers find themselves focused on forcing an outcome rather than helping their toddlers develop healthy habits that will set them on a path to success.

In order to meet the daily suggested sleep guidelines set by the American Academy of Sleep Medicine, toddlers will require at least one nap during their day. Many toddlers naturally wake early sometime between six and eight in the morning. It is quite common for toddlers to take their first nap just a few hours after waking up in the morning, and this can be as long as two hours long. Many toddlers then get sleepy in the afternoon and ready for a mid-afternoon nap in the two o'clock to four o'clock range, and how late parents and caregivers allow for this nap to continue will directly affect bedtime. Common bedtimes for toddlers are typically in the window of time between six and eight pm. For a toddler whose afternoon nap comes closer to the two o'clock time frame, they will likely be ready for bed closer to six o'clock, but the toddler whose afternoon nap falls closer to the four o'clock range, they won't likely be ready for bed until closer to the eight o'clock time frame.

All of these time frames and ranges are estimates, and every child and every family is different. As far as the exact times that will work for you, that will have to be figured out when examining family schedules. The first step in figuring out which sleep schedules will work best for your family is in determining when the ideal time is for your toddler to wake, and when is the ideal time for your toddler to go to sleep at night. Once you have these two times, you can work to structure naps within that time frame as they work for you and your family.

Working within the framework of whatever your family's ideal sleep times will be, there are a couple of different schools of thought on toddler sleep hygiene and what is necessary for our toddlers to get good sleep, and this book will discuss two of them that meet the requirements of loving, respectful discipline, the Attachment Parenting sleep guidance and the RIE sleep guidance for toddlers.

Routine and Rest, Attachment Parenting and RIE

All parents and caregivers will need to figure out what works best for both their toddlers and their families. Some toddlers will sleep best while being gently patted on the back or sang to, and some toddlers will sleep best just being tucked in and kissed goodnight. Our toddlers are no different than we are in this regard. Some people enjoy completely dark and quiet sleep spaces, others need a nightlight and a fan going for white noise. Some people enjoy a very cold bedroom so they can snuggle in under a heavy blanket, while others like their rooms more temperate so they can sleep with a light sheet. Some people like very fluffy, full pillows while others prefer smaller pillows. Sleep is an experience where people have very specific preferences, and our toddlers will have theirs, as well. It is up to parents and caregivers to observe and pay close attention to their toddlers to see what is working best for them and what may be adjusted.

Preparing the sleep space for a calm, relaxing transition into sleep is an important part of creating healthy sleep habits that will hopefully last our little ones their entire lives through. Sleep spaces should be comfortable, and one of the things that may be helpful for parents and caregivers to keep in mind when preparing the sleep space for their toddler, is how most toddlers tend to gravitate towards cozy, smaller spaces. Allowing for fluffy blankets and pillows that can be used to create a cozy nest-like experience can really help our toddlers feel like the space is custom-fitted to them, safe and secure. This is particularly true when switching from the secure boundaries of a crib with sides to an open toddler bed; parents and caregivers can ease this transition by ensuring the toddler bed is a cozy and secure space. Some toddlers find canopies and sleep tents to be especially comforting during this transition.

Some toddlers do very well with one or two of their favorite stuffed animals that can help to serve as a part of their bedtime ritual and reinforcing routine, "Okay, now we need to find your sleepytime stuffy and give him a kiss goodnight. Goodnight, sweet sleepytime stuffy!"

The room that our toddlers are going to be going to sleep in needs to be soothing and calm. Keeping the lights very low during the transition into bedtime will help when all lights are finally turned off (a small nightlight is perfectly fine) and this will help to send the appropriate signals to our toddler's brain that it is time for rest and the sleepy-time hormones will be released.

Routine plays a large part in a loving and respectful transition to bedtime. Create a ritual that works well for your toddler. It is common to have a ritual that goes something like bath time, brush teeth, bedtime story, then bed. Just as the other rituals create a feeling of security and predictability, a bedtime routine is comforting and allows for our toddlers to understand what to expect and to be an active part of the process rather than a passive bystander. There are opportunities here to allow for some autonomy and choice, as well. Parents and caregivers can ask toddlers to choose between two sets of pajamas, to decide if they would like to brush their teeth first or if they would like their parent/caregiver to brush their teeth for them first, or to pick out which book they would like to read. To set your toddler up for success in their choices, it can be helpful to limit how many choices they have, between two or three items. Otherwise, they can become overwhelmed by an entire drawer of pajamas or an entire bookshelf of books and the entire process can become stressful and time-consuming.

Once the bedtime ritual has been established, it should be followed as closely as possible every evening, and even naptimes should have their own ritual. Perhaps it may be modified to drop the bath and the brushing of the teeth, but keep the bedtime story so there is a steady cue present there that reminds the toddler that this is a regular and predictable part of your day. Often times a toddler that may be resistant to the idea of "going to sleep" or "bedtime" may do better with the cue to "rest your body" instead. Tell them that they don't have to go to sleep if they do not want to, but they do have to rest their body, and more often than not, sleep will easily follow. If there is resistance at any point during the bedtime ritual, it is best to honestly and respectfully acknowledge it. "You are saying you do not want to brush your teeth, but it is time for us to brush. Let's brush your teeth so you can pick out your bedtime book. Would you like to brush first, or shall I?" This holds space for our toddler to have their feelings heard and their experience validated, which is often all they need to be able to move on. The same is true for the transition from crib to a "big kid bed," toddlers thrive when their feelings are heard and validated, and when their parents and caregivers give them the support they need for these big transitions.

Attachment Parenting is a parenting style that promotes the creation of strong, healthy, and secure bonds between children and their parents and primary caregivers. Attachment Parenting believes that this can be achieved by keeping children close from infancy through the toddler years, and co-sleeping is often a part of this goal. Co-sleeping may include simply setting up a sleep space in the parent's room, or it may include bedsharing. There is a strong evolutionary and physiological rationale behind co-sleeping, as it is the way that mammals have slept since the dawn of time, and continue to do so in most cultures around the world. The advent of separate, contained sleep spaces such as we see in modern society with babies and toddlers in their own rooms, separated from the rest of the family, is fairly new in historical terms. For young babies, up to six months of age, there is a protective effect against SIDS that is found from sharing a sleep space, and it is hypothesized that sharing a sleep space allows for the infant to better regulate their respiratory systems to those they share a sleep space with. It is also very helpful for breastfeeding relationships to have infants sleeping nearby, as it is less disruptive to both the infant and the breastfeeding parent for nighttime feeds. As babies morph into toddlers, there is no immediate desire to separate from this co-sleeping arrangement that occurs from the arbitrary date on the calendar that marks them as now officially a toddler, so many toddlers are more than happy to continue on in this arrangement throughout the toddler years. If toddlers and their parents and caregivers are still happy to continue this arrangement, there is no harm in waiting until toddlers are ready to move from the shared sleep space.

Many co-sleeping families arrange their beds so they are nearby, such as having a crib "side-car" where one of the cribs sides have been removed so it can act as an extension to the main bed. That particular arrangement allows for the baby/toddler to have their own space but still be very close. Some co-sleeping families have a crib or toddler bed in the same room, and some opt for a "floor bed," which is often just a toddler size mattress on the floor near the main bed. These options all keep the child in the same room with their parents, and sleep is a shared event. For babies and toddlers that are co-sleeping, sometimes they might desire more cuddling and physical comfort as they are drifting off to sleep, as this is what they are used to. Co-sleeping advocates point out that this is not typically so different from what most adults enjoy, too, as most adults that share a bed with another adult also enjoy a bit of a cuddle before drifting off as well.

Parents and caregivers following Attachment Parenting principles will likely stay with their toddler as they are drifting off to sleep, perhaps patting them on the back, singing lullabies, telling stories in a low, calm voice, or even just snuggling into them and allowing them to drift off to sleep by their side.

RIE guidelines for toddler sleep are less hands-on than Attachment Parenting sleep guidelines.

RIE is a philosophy that stands for Respect in Infant Educarers, but the RIE principles are extended beyond infancy to toddlers and older children as well. At its core, RIE principles are founded in respect for and trust in children that they are able to be successful in their lives. In regards to sleep, RIE proposes that parents and caregivers place more trust in their toddlers and that once the sleep environment has been set up and the toddler has been placed in their bed, it is up to the parent/caregiver to give appropriate space to the toddler to drift off to sleep by themselves.

RIE sleep principles are sometimes confused with "cry it out" philosophy that encourages parents to let their babies and toddlers cry themselves to sleep if they are upset about being put to bed. RIE distinguishes itself from this particularly harsh theory by stating that their goal is to allow toddlers the freedom to have their big feelings and express them by crying, and to offer verbal support and encouragement reminding our toddlers that we believe they are able and capable of going to sleep.

An integral part of the RIE sleep guidelines is consistency. If a toddler makes their way from their bed into the parent's, the parent must get up and walk them back to their bed every time in order to maintain the consistency that is needed for the toddler to understand what to expect. Just as routine provides security and predictability for toddlers during their waking hours, RIE believes that this security and predictability at night is especially important so that babies and toddlers learn they can be confident they are capable of putting themselves to sleep without needing the external assistance from parents and caregivers. RIE believes that children thrive with boundaries, and the boundaries around bedtime allow toddlers to be able to relax and unwind into sleep without angst.

RIE differs from Attachment Parenting sleep guidelines dramatically in their stance about co-sleeping. RIE does not believe co-sleeping ever sets up future healthy sleep habits and states that children should be given their own separate sleep space and to be put down to bed by themselves and left to put themselves to sleep from infancy forward. RIE sleep guidelines state that it does the child more good to be a confident leader that places the child down in their bed and then trusts them to learn how to settle themselves down. RIE believes that some crying taking place at bedtime is a necessary part of the process in decompressing from their day and also functions as their communication to their parents and caregivers that they have big feelings around the experience, but that a part of trusting them and equipping them with tools for future healthy sleep habits is allowing them to work through these big feelings on their own. RIE advocates that toddlers should not be left to scream themselves to sleep, but if given the space and time to get their big feelings and tears out, they will settle themselves and have learned that they are capable of doing so.

Above all, both Attachment Parenting and RIE both believe that a consistent and predictable routine help our toddlers to have a secure and comfortable relationship with bedtime. Both schools of thought encourage parents and caregivers to carefully observe what is happening with your toddler and to understand that behavior is always communication. If your toddler is screaming at the top of their lungs at bedtime each night, there is a need there that has not been met. Is there a physical issue such as acid reflux or teething that needs addressed? Does your toddler have a fear of the dark that a simple nightlight could help with? Are you rushing through the bedtime rituals so quickly that your toddler feels the tension and carries it with them to bed and can't settle because they aren't sure what the tension was about? Sleep isn't something parents and caregivers have to "fix" or force, once the environment and the routine has been remedied, sleep will come. If it does not, or if intuition is telling you that something is still not quite right, please seek the advice of your pediatrician to ensure that there is not something physical that has been overlooked.

Toddlers and Tech

Toddlers and tech has been a significant part of the parenting conversation since portable technology use has skyrocketed in recent years. The American Academy of Pediatrics still recommends no screen time for children younger than eighteen months, other than video-chatting on apps such as Skype or FaceTime. For children between the ages of two and five, they suggest limiting screen time to one hour per day and only of high-quality programs. This may seem excessively cautious as we live in a world where most adults spend most of their days with one hand on their portable tech devices, but there is good reason for this caution. Among toddlers who use hand-held mobile tech devices, the more time spent with these tech devices, the more likely they are to have delayed speech skills. In fact, a recent study showed that for every thirty-minute increase of screen time, there was a 49% increase risk in expressive speech delay! There are other areas of concern, as well. Sitting down and watching a TV show in the family room is a passive activity, and any activity that encourages a child to slow down their physical movement, their cognitive engagement, and their creativity, is best to only allow in moderation, but interacting with tech through hand-held devices such as tablets carries additional risk by means of the sheer nature of the product. Hand-held tech devices go everywhere with us, and are often used to placate and distract toddlers in scenarios such as waiting rooms, restaurants, and in their car seats. This is leading to a generation of children that are not developing important life skills such as patience. There is a need for toddlers to be able to interact with the world around them, and interacting with a screen is not the same as engaging socially with the people around you. There has also been connections drawn between dwindling attention spans and heavy tech use in children.

As with all new things- and this hand-held heavy tech use by young children is still fairly new- it is usually wise to have caution. In guiding and teaching our toddlers in a loving and respectful way, it is important to directly engage with them as we help them to build important skills such as patience, waiting their turn, and interacting socially, as opposed to handing them distraction in a screen.

Useful Information and Tips for This Chapter

8 Common Mistakes in Child Feeding

Mistake 1: Forcing the kid to eat

If you are forcing your child to eat something he does not like, think about this method again. This way of feeding can tire both you and your child, and the negative consequences are numerous because then you will not only disgust food for him but the whole ritual and the time of eating. Instead, do not pay attention when a child does not like something to eat. If you have not made a pomp about this, the next time a child eats the same food, they will not oppose that much. In time and with your positive attitude, it will start quite normally to eat that food.

Mistake 2: Preparing only what the child loves!

Many parents fall into the trap of preparing only the child's favorite food, precisely because of the fear that it will stay hungry. However, this is not a solution. Instead, prepare him a meal containing at least one of his favorite ingredients. For example, if your child likes to eat only fries and meat, and hesitates from vegetables, you prepare a meal with one of the ingredients he likes and one that he doesn't. If the child is older include him in food preparation, it will certainly motivate him to try everything!

Mistake 3: Insisting that the child eats everything on the plate

Parents are mostly overdosing the portions. If you can not determine the size of a portion yourself, seek professional advice. The practice is to serve one tablespoon in accordance with the child's age for each ingredient. For example, pour two tablespoons of rice, carrots and some meat for a two-year-old child. It is important that the child has had a snack an hour or two before the main meal. Instead of making your child to eat everything on the plate, make sure that it is full-fed and satisfied.

Mistake 4: Ignoring the child's taste preferences

Children have a much more elaborate pallet than adults (which eventually disappears). Something that is not salty or spicy enough for you, for your child may be too salty and too spicy. Make sure you cook mild food for your child and listen when it tells you that his food is too spicy.

Mistake 5: Giving up too soon

Do not give up easily if a child refuses food on the first try. According to research, it is necessary to offer the child approximately 20 times the same food before it is accepted. Instead of giving up on certain foods, prepare these foods and allow the child to play with it. This implies touching it, as well as placing it in the mouth and spit it out afterward. In time they will accept a particular food and will no longer make a problem.

Mistake 6: Sweets

Sweets are not good for adults, let alone as a snack for your children. Such a snack is full of sugar, artificial colors and additives that are in no way good for health. Instead of sweets, offer your child some fruit or some other healthy food.

Mistake 7: Food as a reward

If you use some not so healthy foods such as sweets or snacks as a reward for finished meal, you're mistaken! This way you will easily develop a bad eating habit in your child. Adding candy as a reward can also develop an addiction. Instead with food, reward your child by taking him to a park or with some other favorite activity.

Mistake 8: Caution with juices

It is recommended that the child drinks about half a glass of 100 percent juice per day. A larger quantity than recommended only creates sugar deposits, which in turn affects the absence of appetite in the child. The tip is to replace the juices with water. If the child loves the juice that much then dilute it with water.

Common Sleep Mistakes Parents Make

Skipping a bedtime routine

Routine helps your baby to relax, and that's also a nice way for you to get closer to your child. An hour before you want your baby to fall asleep begin with the selected routine. A warm bath can help relax your baby, then place it in a darkened room and let her lie down, or better yet, read her a story.

Ignoring the signs of fatigue

It is very important to see signs that show that the baby is tired. Some of these signs are: rubbing the eyes, yawning, slowing activity, nervousness, loss of interest for people and play. If you miss out on those signs that occur when your baby's sleeping time comes, his body will not produce a calming hormone-melatonin. Instead, the adrenal gland will produce hormones that are associated with stress and the baby will be nervous and irritable. These signs always appear at the same time.

Moving from crib to bed too soon

This is a classic mistake that parents make. Do not move your child to bed until it can get out of the crib on its own. This is the moment when the child is ready for a classic bed.

Letting your child sleep wherever

Napping in a children's carriage, in a child seat for a car or a feeder, is not good, because the child does not fall into a deep and quiet sleep. In order to develop a habit for quality sleep, the child should be in a lying position and in a familiar zone where he usually sleeps every day.

You do not have a clearly defined sleep schedule

Children need regular sleep time both during the day and at night, in order to regulate the day and night hormonal cycles. It is good for children to know the exact time of going to bed and to make it a habit. It is therefore important that parents respect that time.

The child remains awake till late because parents believe he will sleep longer

The children inner clock is so powerful that it awakens them in the morning at about the same time, no matter when they go to bed. Parents who allow their little ones to stay awake for a long time can in fact only get a counter effect. The child will be exhausted and nervous the next day.

Parents are not on the same side when raising a child

They must be united when the child is growing up, especially when it comes to improving his sleep. They should be unanimous when it comes to tactics they will apply when child relaxing and sleeping is in question.

Giving up too soon

It's never too late to change bad habits. Parents need to be patient. Nothing changes overnight, that also means bad habits.

TEMPER TANTRUMS: BIG FEELINGS STRATEGY

Parents and caregivers know all too well that tantrums are just a part of the territory for toddlers, aren't they? One of the reasons for this is due in part to what was already mentioned previously; there is a new and exciting world all around them, full of things to see and explore, but they can't seem to get their little hands and bodies to cooperate fully to explore them, can't seem to understand fully why things are the way they are, and are told "no" often. This can be a very frustrating stage of development and toddlers love to express their frustration in BIG ways with BIG feelings.

Big feelings is a phrase that can be used to help parents and caregivers remember that when toddlers are acting out in temper tantrums, it is often a result of them experiencing such a rush of powerful emotions, desires, and needs that they are unable to deal with and process themselves, that they explode into what we call a temper tantrum. It is the physical manifestation of their frustration and angst, and it is often well-justified. The ability and the skill to safely handle strong emotions in a healthy manner is one that some adults are even still working on!

There are many ways in which parents and caregivers are able to help their toddlers further develop their emotional control and ability to handle their big feelings, but that all falls apart if the parents and caregivers themselves are unable to walk the walk.

Modeling and demonstrating how to handle our own big feelings such as frustration, anger, and disappointment are the building blocks of how our toddlers figure out how to manage their own big feelings. If a toddler watches their parents or caregivers loudly yell at the car in front of them for cutting them off in rush hour traffic, or sees their parents engage angrily with each other regularly over the dinner table, then these behaviors will be internalized by the toddler as appropriate behavior. It is unfortunate that often times in our society, we end up holding small children to a higher standard than we do ourselves. Most adults can remember the last time they were angry about something and let a door slam as a physical release for that anger, but yet heaven help us if our three-year-old child would do the same, we would feel the need to intervene and put a stop to that behavior immediately, often labeling it as "bad." It is this sort of double standard that must be honestly looked at when we are raising small children. Toddlers are very monkey see, monkey do, and they will do what they see their most trusted and beloved adult influences in their lives do. For most toddlers, this is their parents and the caregivers they see and interact with the most.

In order to better manage our own emotions, it is important for adults to remember that sometimes it is through the process of having children that we discover the pieces of ourselves that need attention. It is far easier to suppress our own big feelings by means of self-medicating through unhealthy behaviors such as binge-eating and alcohol use before we have children, but once children arrive it can be the much needed impetus to take a good, long, hard look at ourselves and make the move to unpack our own personal baggage and work on the parts of ourselves that need work. There is great benefit to this, beside the obvious light at the end of the tunnel in which we are a more well-adjusted person, but there is also providing the model for our children that no one is perfect, and everyone is working to become the best versions of themselves.

In fact, this is an important part of providing loving and respectful discipline to toddlers. Everyone slips up from time to time, and when a parent or caregiver makes a mistake with a toddler-whether it be by raising their voice needlessly or making a poor judgement call about something out of haste, it is incredibly important that the parent or caregiver take the time to specifically say to the toddler that they are sorry, and they are working to do better. This is something that all children need to hear from their parents and caregivers. Not only is it modeling to our children that we are all a work in progress and no one is perfect all of the time, but it also provides a unique opportunity for our children to offer us something special: grace. Indeed, toddlers are able to do this beautifully, and the relationship between parents, caregivers, and toddler are strengthened by this experience.

There is a powerful saying that can be helpful to keep handy and visible during the toddler years, perhaps written on a white board or on a slip of paper stuck to the fridge with a magnet, but somewhere that can remind parents and caregivers while they are riding out a toddler temper tantrum, and it is this: "Bring the calm to their storm." The picture here is that they already have a storm happening inside of them. They are already wild, chaotic, and uncontrolled. The very last thing they would ever need would be their most trusted adult figures, their parents and their caregivers, to come at them with their own storm energy. Instead of contributing to their chaos, it is up to us as parents and caregivers to bring an energy that calms. What this may look like is going to be different for each toddler and each individual scenario, but the basic tenets will remain the same.

Empathize with your toddler. It is helpful to work on feeling the authentic experience of empathy rather than just attempting to perform it. True empathy is an understanding of where another person is coming from and how it might feel to be in the very situation they find themselves in. When speaking of empathy for our toddlers and how to feel what it might be like to be in the situation they find themselves in, this is obviously not on a superficial level. It may be hard as an adult to have much empathy for a situation in which the basic grievance being aired involves getting the red cup instead of the blue cup with lunch, but as parents and caregivers that are pursuing loving and respectful discipline, you will know that it is about so much more. At the basis of a temper tantrum surrounding a scenario like that, is the lack of autonomy and the lack of control over their own lives. As was discussed previously in this book, toddlers are living lives that are mostly out of their control. Their days are planned out for them from the moment they awake until the moment they go to bed. They do not get to choose what they wear, what they eat, where they go, or who is caring for them. For the most part, they do not get to do the things they want to do (like play in the dog's water dish) or go where they want to go, and it surely must be a frustrating experience to be surrounded by so many interesting things that you are hardwired to explore by touching and tasting but you are denied this opportunity by people that are bigger than you and more capable than you.

This may seem like a stretch or an unnecessary exercise in trying to better handle your toddler's temper tantrums, but rest assured that it is not. Empathizing is what allows parents and caregivers to take their toddler's big feelings seriously. It is all too easy to trivialize the upsets and frustrations of toddlers from an adult vantage point, but it is important to remember that they do not have an adult vantage point, and to them their upsets and their frustrations are a very big deal. In fact, if parents and caregivers trivialize their toddlers big feelings, it can create a relationship where children grow up to believe that their big feelings are not worth sharing with the trusted adults in their life, and this is how it can become a habit for children to turn away from their parents with their big feelings as they go through middle school and high school. Most parents and caregivers want children in their care to feel comfortable and safe bringing them their concerns, and this feeling of comfort and safety begins at a very young age.

Once parents and caregivers are able to truly empathize with their toddlers, it is important to let the toddler know that they are heard, they are understood, and their parent/caregiver is there for them. Unfortunately, parents and caregivers are often quick to try to jump in and "fix" whatever is causing the temper tantrum, but an important part of this process involves giving the space- providing that it is a safe space in which the toddler can not hurt themselves or others- for them to work through their big feelings and come back to a calm and reasonable level.

One way that a parent or a caregiver can attempt to keep a temper tantrum from escalating is by sportscasting, or helping the toddler to feel understood by naming the emotions they may be experiencing, and demonstrating to them that you see what has happened. It might look something like this, "Oh, I see. You wanted the red cup, but I put your juice in the blue cup. Yes, that would be frustrating. I am sorry," or "You really want to get the dog's water dish! You like playing in the water, but I'm telling you "no" because that is the dog's water." Sportscasting is ensuring that not only does your toddler hear that you understand what is happening with them, but they are also learning how to identify and articulate their emotions. They are learning language at an incredible speed, and being able to accurately describe their emotional state will go a long way towards guiding them to a healthy ability to deal with and handle their emotions.

When parents and caregivers use key terms such as, "I hear you," and "I know," and "I saw that…" toddlers are able to feel like while they may not get their way, they are at the very least, not being ignored or dismissed. No one likes to be ignored or dismissed.

Parents and caregivers are responsible for ensuring that toddlers have a safe space to work through their big feelings, but there need not be a rush to "stop the temper tantrum," as this can be a much-needed release of pent-up frustration and angst. As your toddler is getting this pent-up frustration out, it is necessary for parents and caregivers to stay close. One reason for this is because parents and caregivers never want to send the message to their toddlers that their big feelings are too much for them to handle. It is already too much for their toddler to handle, as is evidenced by the temper tantrum, but the idea that it is also too much to handle for their most trusted and depended upon adults, would be unsettling. It is important to remain close and to continue providing calm words of affirmation such as, "I hear you, that was tough," or "yes, you are very upset right now." Some toddlers respond well to their parents and caregivers trying to rub their backs or asking for a hug, as these physical touches can help to settle them physiologically. Others may well need to finish getting the temper tantrum energy out before being able to connect physically with their parents and caregivers.

Always, when the temper tantrum has lost its steam, parents and caregivers need to reconnect with their toddlers. Get down to their level, either kneeling or sitting close to them. Reach out for their hands if they will let you and let them know that you are always there for them, that you love them no matter what, and that you understand that what they just went through was difficult. This reconnection between adults, caregivers, and toddlers is what allows toddlers to be able to process what just happened. It can be helpful to remind yourself that your toddler was not trying to give you a hard time, your toddler was having a hard time. Recall that toddlers do not want to be at odds with their parents and caregivers, but they are still new to this world and have a lot to learn. It is our job as parents and caregivers to help guide and teach them.

It can be helpful to retrace the steps before the temper tantrum so we can learn what can be changed to try and avoid a repeat performance. If the temper tantrum inducing experience was about the dog's water dish, then perhaps it is time to move the dog's water dish where it is completely out of the toddler's reach, as your toddler is showing you again and again that they are not ready to handle the temptation of the dog's water dish or the frustration that comes with being denied it. If the temper tantrum inducing experience was about the blue cup being given to them instead of the red cup, consider if perhaps the entire debacle could have been avoided by offering the choice of choosing which color cup before pouring the juice? Sometimes there are very simple adjustments that can be made in how we relate to our toddlers that can save both them and their parents and caregivers a lot of frustration.

Once a toddler is in the middle of their expression of their big feelings… aka a temper tantrum… it can be tempting for parents and caregivers to try to do anything they can in that moment to stop the temper tantrum. This is not necessarily the healthiest way to guide and teach our toddler how to make their way out of this headspace. There will be times, of course, when this is a necessity. For example, if a toddler is having an epic temper tantrum in the middle of a crowded movie theater because they were denied more M&M's, then yes, of course, hand over more of the M&M's and consider it a lesson learned in the volatility of what must be expected when taking toddlers to public spaces with expectations such as that. However, each temper tantrum provides parents and caregivers a unique opportunity to see what it is that our toddlers are dealing with and how they are handling things. When temper tantrums are occurring daily, or even multiple times per day, this is an excellent communication on the part of your child that something else is awry.

Parents and caregivers must look at all behavior as communication. Toddlers are not able to articulate advanced needs eloquently by stating something like, "I'm worried about my Grandma because she has been sick for a long time and people speak in hushed tones about her around me but I don't really understand what that means other than I can't see her as often as I used to," or "I've been stressed out lately because all of our things are being boxed up and everyone keeps talking about how we are moving to a new house, but I don't really understand what that means so I'm nervous and afraid about where all of our things are going." A toddler that is experiencing frequent temper tantrums is communicating to their parents and caregivers that something is happening with them that is unsettling or confusing. It will be up to parents and caregivers to examine what is going on in the household, in the care environment, with the toddler physically, in order to know how to address this with their toddler. Toddlers need reassurance during times of transition in the household, and a simple but confident explanation from parents and caregivers can go a long way to helping them feel secure again. For example, all that may be needed is for one of their trusted adults to remind them that, "Yes, Grandma has been sick for a while now, hasn't she? We will go see her as soon as she gets better," or "We are putting all of our stuff into boxes so we can take everything with us when we move. It will be so fun to open them all back up at our new house, won't it?" Toddlers thrive with reassurances like these in unsettling times. They are more aware of their surroundings than what adults what to give them credit for sometimes!

All in all, temper tantrums will remain a part of life for toddler children regardless of how parents and caregivers arrange their environment or handle their feelings, because toddlers are simply unequipped to handle big feelings and frustrations in a more controlled manner at this age. That is okay, and developmentally appropriate. What parents and caregivers should always be aiming to do is to better understand what is behind the big feelings and frustrations and how they might be able to assist their toddler in either relieving themselves of some of these frustrations and how to release them safely. If there has been a steady increase in frequency or severity, then it is detective time for parents and caregivers to carefully observe and ensure that there is nothing more that can be done to help their toddlers feel more safe and secure, and if there is nothing there but parents and caregivers still find themselves concerned about the frequency or severity, then it is up to them to look to medical and behavioral health professionals to ensure that there is not an additional reason that their toddler may be having a hard time processing their big feelings.

Useful Information and Tips for This Chapter

Typical situations in which a child experiences tantrums

Teddy bear your three-year-old child took to the kindergarten had disappeared. He was looking for him with a teacher, but they didn't manage to find him. When he realized that he had to go home without the teddy, he began hysterically to cry and kick his feet on the floor. In this situation, the child's behavior should not be ignored, because he faces the loss of something important and requires consolation, compassion. It's best to hug him and when he calms down, you say: "You're sad because your teddy had disappeared. How can I help you? "So you make it clear that you understand and sympathize with him, that you are there for him, and teach him how to name what he feels.

The toy box of your three-year-old daughter is up in the closet. You refuse to take down the box: "The box is now up there because you didn't pick up the toys after play." Suddenly she burst into tears and screaming, but you should not give in. If you give in and satisfy her just to stop the outburst of anger, then the tantrum might become a regular phenomenon because she will realize that this behavior leads to the goal. Ignore her outburst of anger by continuing your activities and not paying attention to her, but keep an eye on her and don't leave her alone in the room, especially if the tantrum is very intense and if she is inclined to hurt herself and others in those situations.

A two-year-old child understands more than he can say in words. He has his own need that he can't express and feels frustrated. Instead with words, he expresses his frustration with the outburst of anger. For example. you brought your child a glass of yogurt because he expressed a desire to drink yogurt, but he angrily says, "I don't want it," and begins to cry suddenly. You say: "Okay. You do not want yogurt "and take the glass. You come back from the kitchen, and your child is hitting the table with fists and shouts furiously: "Yooogurt, give me, give me, give me yogurt!" You assume he probably wants a fruit yogurt, but he doesn't know how to say. If you immediately bring him the fruit yogurt and fulfill his desire, it's harder for tantrums to disappear by themselves, as the child will realize that this behavior is worthwhile and leads to the goal. He'll expect you to read his mind next time and run to get what he wants. In addition, in this way, you do not encourage him to adopt new words, because why would he try to learn to say it if his mom brings what he wants as soon as he cries. It is best to move your child to a more peaceful place so he can't push down or break what's on the table. Tell him: "When you stop screaming, I will come to you." During the tantrums the child can't hear you, nor can he reasonably think, so there is no point in trying to talk. Only when the child calms down say, "When you scream, I don't know what you want. Let's go to the refrigerator so you can show me what you want "... As the child grows, so does the speech skills and the level of frustration decreases, and the outbursts of anger become less frequent.

Your two-and-a-half-year-old son is trying to put on his socks, but he can't, and starts kicking his feet and crying. In an effort to give him support and comfort, you tried to hug him and say, "You almost succeeded, do you want me to help?" This angers him even more and he pushes you with the words: "I'll do it alone, I want to do it on my own, alone, let meee! "In this situation, it's important to stay patient. Let him blow off some steam, but let him know that you are there if he needs you: "Okay, I'll be on the couch, call me if you need me." Only when he calms down and asks for your help, advise him how can he easily put on the socks, and if you see that he can't do it himself, help him. This way you teach him how to overcome obstacles, send him a message you believe in him, to be persistent, it is okay to seek help and you'll be there for him.

You drive a car. A one-year-old is in his child car seat. Suddenly he begins to swing with his hands and feet and scream hysterically. It may be hungry, thirsty, tired, having a wet diaper, being too hot, feeling uncomfortable in the seat, angry that you stopped, because he doesn't understand that you have to stop on the red light, maybe he does not like the music you have just put on, he just want you to take him, he wants your attention ... It is not always easy to determine the cause of the tantrum, but the elimination of the cause of the tantrum (if the cause is the wet diaper, the tantrum will stop when you change the child) or preventing the appearance of tantrums (if you notice that the child begins with the tantrum whenever a certain song comes on, skip it) are the solution to this situation.

You went to a relative who has twins of twelve months. Your four-year-old son suddenly angrily asks: "When are we going home?" You answer: "In half an hour." Suddenly a child begins to roll on the floor and scream: "Oh, not again, in half an hour, noo ..." In this situation, it is best to take your four-year-old into another room (because he gives a bad example to younger children and can get someone hurt) and tell him that the conversation is possible only when he stops screaming. Your attempts to talk to a child while in tantrum state will be unsuccessful because the child is so overwhelmed by emotions that he can't hear you, process information, and think reasonably.

When the child stops screaming, talk about what happened and tell him what he supposed to do in similar situations: "Okay, it's boring, but that doesn't mean you should roll on the floor and scream. If you want my attention, if you want me to sit beside you and play, then tell me it's enough, you do not need to roll around on the floor and scream. "In this way you teach him to solve problems with conversation and that rage can be controlled by turning it into words. Keep in mind that older children often consciously use tantrums to have it their way or to get attention, because they've realized that parents react to this behavior and that it's a convenient way to achieve the goal so the tantrum can become a form of behavior in later life. These are the so-called manipulative tantrums.

In time, as the child grows, it becomes more independent, more skillful, more mature, his perception of himself and the world develops, teaches him to express needs in an adequate way, expresses feelings with words, and the tantrums become rarer. In the meantime, do not forget to pay attention to the child even when it behaves acceptable, to hug and love him when he is joyful, and not only when it needs consolation.

Basic Rules to Prevent Tantrums

When a child has a tantrum, then three basic things work: your presence, calmness, and language of emotion.

1. Once the tantrum starts, there is often nothing we can do to stop it immediately.

What you can do is reduce the intensity and with your support and presence, in the long run, help the child gain self-regulation.

2. Stay present and calm.

Even though the child seems to fight you, it's necessary that you remain present and calm. As much as these situations can be disturbing, keep in mind the following:

• it's a normal phase and the way of expressing accumulated feelings and frustrations during childhood,

• the outbreaks of anger are not personal, and the child doesn't do that to you intentionally

• when a child is upset, he needs a calm and stable adult who will help him restore his own emotional security. If both the child and the parent are raging in that situation, then you have a double problem.

3. Communicate with emotions.

When we are emotional, we can't understand anything else. When you describe how the child is feeling, you are addressing his emotional part of the brain that can hear you and the child has the feeling that you understand him.

"This is very difficult for you now." "It angers you; I understand." "You're sad because you can't get that toy. You really want it. I know "examples are how we can show understanding and remain calm and present.

It's really important to try to connect. If these sentences are expressed as a child control technique, the child feels that and the outbreak is even stronger.

4. Feelings are slow, give them time.

5. Do not force your child into physical contact in the first stage.

When kids are angry and have an outburst, they often want to distance themselves and refuse physical contact. This is totally normal behavior when we get angry at someone. So, don't force yourself and don't insist on physical contact and hugs in the first stage of the outbreak when the anger and fury in the child are growing. But don't leave him alone because your child needs you very much and you need to stay as close as you can.

If your child hits you, wants to hurt himself or break something, then take him, hold him in your arms and say something like This is not safe. I will not let you do what's not safe. I know it's hard. Sometimes it takes some time for a child to calm down, sometimes you need to repeat several times, but it's good news that this first stage, when the rage is growing, always passes.

6. Offer contact when the child is ready.

When this emotional storm reaches its peak, the child is ready for contact. Often at that moment, they start crying sadly, sob, look at us or in some other way they let us know they are ready for contact. Encourage a child, hug him and let him calm down in your arms. This is not the time for lectures and lessons. Stay with your child and say something like This was very hard. It's all right now. I'm here.

7. Carefully observe.

With careful observation, you will be able to see what are the typical triggers and situations which starts the outbreaks. Is that the inability to get what he wants? Too much stimulation? Hunger? Exhaustion or shopping centers? Then sometimes we can prevent them and react to the first signs. There is a greater chance that an outbreak will not occur or it will be smaller.

If you can't recognize the pattern, it's possible there are many things that are accumulating and come out at one moment.

8. Accept the illogical nature of tantrums.

Yes, they are illogical. Yes, they will happen regardless of the fact that your child promised to behave. And yes, they will repeat - how often and fiercely, it depends on the child's temperament, the ability of self-regulation and external support.

9. Tantrums are a normal form of expressing feelings in early childhood.

Because of immaturity, undeveloped nerve system and emotional instability, children have no other way to deal with frustrations, challenges, desires, intense development.

10. If they become more frequent or oftentimes occur with older children, it means we reward them somehow.

PUNISHMENT: WHAT IT DOES

Finally, we come to punishment. For most parents and caregivers, punishment is often considered to be synonymous with physical punishment and the infliction of pain and discomfort to influence behavior, and there is much more to loving and respectful discipline than this.

Punishment falls under the umbrella of operant conditioning, or the placement of consequences to influence behavior. The four types of conditioning are positive punishment, positive reinforcement, negative punishment, and negative reinforcement. A simplistic way to view these is that punishment seeks to discourage a behavior while reinforcement is about encouraging a behavior. A positive is when something is added to influence behavior, while a negative is when something is taken away to influence behavior.

Positive Punishment

This is when a consequence is added to influence and often discourage a behavior. An example of this is spanking a child for poor behavior. A consequence (physical pain) was added to influence behavior.

Positive Reinforcement

This is when a consequence is added to encourage a behavior, such as a reward of ice cream for a job well done at the doctor's office. Something was added (ice cream) to encourage more of the behavior that the parent/caregiver would like to see.

Negative Punishment

This is when something is taken away to influence behavior, such as cancelling a fun outing due to poor behavior at home. Something was taken away (the fun outing) to discourage the poor behavior at home.

Negative Reinforcement

This is when something unpleasant is removed to reinforce a behavior, such as stopping nagging your toddler to begin cleaning up his blocks if he will instead pick up only ten blocks. You've removed the expectation that they must clean up all of the blocks and encouraged them to pick up some.

Which One is Best?

This is a bit of a loaded question, because various forms of punishment and reinforcement can have a variety of outcomes at different times and in different scenarios in a child's life. There are some absolutes, however. While controversial to some who still practice it, physical punishment such as spanking, hitting, smacking, popping, or slapping has very real and very negative consequences for children. Over fifty years of thorough research into physical punishment has revealed that it is closely associated with negative outcomes such as increased aggression, antisocial behavior, physical injuries, and mental health problems. In fact, physical punishment such as spanking has been determined to be such a dangerous disciplinary method that it has been banned around the world by over thirty countries, and even more telling, these countries with full bans on physical punishment have significantly lower rates of violence among children and adults. When we take into consideration how much parents and caregivers are the primary models for our young children, showing them how to behave and interact with the world around them, it seems quite obvious that children who are met with violence in their earliest years will internalize the message that violence is an acceptable tool to use throughout their lives.

At its very core, using physical pain as a tool to "teach" requires the assumption that we cannot teach out children without inflicting pain. The experience of toddlers having pain inflicted upon them by their most trusted and respected adults, their parents and their caregivers, disrupts the relationship of trust and security that is so important to a child's foundation of a strong sense of self and self-esteem. Being physically afraid of the person you depend on and count on to meet your every need is toxic. It is just as toxic for a small child as it is for a spouse that is physically afraid of their significant other, except a toddler will have absolutely no means of escape or opportunity to leave the abuse, and their brains are growing and developing while existing in that state of perpetual fear.

Beyond all of the negative physical, mental and emotional outcomes, there is the sometimes-unexpected reality that it is ineffective. Physical pain punishment such as spanking may often stop the behavior in the moment, but it does not teach the child the preferred behavior and often leaves them in a headspace where they are unable to truly grasp whatever lesson their parent/caregiver was attempting to teach. If spanking "worked," then a parent who spanked would not need to continue to dole out spankings, but this is not the case and is one of the reasons why spanking is associated with child abuse. In order to gain the same fearful outcome and impact as a child ages, parents must use increased force and strength, and this can easily lead to significant physical injuries in the name of discipline. Another way to consider the effectiveness of spanking is this: If you spank your toddler because they were pulling the dogs tail, would you spank once and then be satisfied and confident that your toddler would not do it again? Most would agree that no, this would not be the case. This is because especially in the early toddler years when toddlers have very little impulse control due to the under-formed prefrontal cortex of their brains as they are still growing and developing, it is impossible for them to have this self-control. All of the spanking in the world cannot expedite the growth and development of this part of the brain, but it can instead replace it with an extreme fear of exploration. When this happens, a parent or caregiver may feel they've gotten through to their toddler, but this could not be further from the truth. All that has happened is that the toddler has been trained into a submission akin to the training of an animal. Our toddlers deserve better than this, most parents and caregivers would agree.

Angry verbal chastisement such as yelling and lecturing intensely (we all can see the picture, adult bent over wagging an angry finger in their small child's face) is also considered to be a part of this physical pain punishment spectrum, and the fear and stress chemicals released in the brain during this experience for toddlers are the exact same ones released during physical pain punishment such as spanking. Verbal abuse leaves its scars, too. A parent that finds themselves resorting to yelling and angry words on a regular basis needs to realize that this says more about where they are with their own anger management and emotional control than how their toddler is behaving.

So, if physical pain punishment such as spanking is off the table, what's left? Plenty!

Loving and respectful discipline often begins with a shift in perspective on the part of the parent and caregiver. Discipline does not need to hurt and punish in order to affect behavioral change, in fact the longest lasting behavioral changes are often a result of positive parenting principles such as modeling, positive reinforcement, and natural consequences. We know that modeling to our toddlers how we would like them to be and behave is an exemplary way to lovingly and respectfully guide and teach them what we would like to see. Positive reinforcement, or the addition of something to reinforce the behavior you want to see is effective in that it gives our children something to continue to work towards. This may look something like this: Your toddler is having a hard time avoiding pulling your purse down from the counter. You have found them several times, pulling the purse down and emptying out its contents. Positive reinforcement would be essentially catching your toddler in the act of doing what they are supposed to do rather than what they are not supposed to do. In this case, it would be seeing your toddler walk towards the purse on the counter, notice it there, and continue walking past. Parents and caregivers would need to notice this in a big way, "oh look at you! You are being such a big kid! You saw mommy's purse and knew that you are not supposed to touch it, so you walked right past it and left it alone. Awesome job, big kid!" and this could be accompanied by a physical positive reinforcement such as a hug or a high five. This will often be accompanied by the toddler then moving forward to test this new behavior, so perhaps the next time they walk towards the purse and lean forward and poke it with a finger.

Parents/caregivers would need to correct this verbally by reminding the toddler that no, they are not supposed to touch it, and then they need to be keeping a close eye to "catch" the toddler making the right choice again to repeat the positive enforcement and really ensure that the lesson is being absorbed. This is not a one and done fix, but nothing with our tiny toddlers is. They are learning and developing and need our patience as we work to help them develop themselves into the best they can be.

An underrated tool in the loving and respectful discipline toolbox is the use and allowance of natural consequences. This differs from artificially imposed consequences. A natural consequence of a bad behavior might be if we have told our toddler repeatedly that they must come into the bedroom to get dressed, but they are absorbed in playing and repeatedly say "no" when you tell them to come get dressed. Around the age of two and a half to three years old, toddlers will be able to grasp more "if, then" concepts such as, "if you don't come get dressed, we won't be able to go to the park today," and so allowing this natural consequence to play out is an effective way to show toddlers that there are results to their actions. This also plays into their sense of autonomy and choice, as when they are told that they can not go to the park because they did not get dressed in time, they will hear that they were the ones in control of the situation. Again, this will not be an immediate lesson or a one and done form of discipline, but it is guiding and teaching toddlers to understand that they have responsibility for their actions.

There is another disciplinary tactic that is commonly used in our society: the time out. Interesting brain research done at UCLA revealed that brain scans of children being placed in time out look the same as children being subjected to physical pain. There has been debate about the various ways that time out can look and how it may be used in a loving and respectful manner as a way to encourage children to center themselves. Time out that is excessively punitive is often considered to be time out that lasts for extended periods of time (anything beyond a five minute mark for a small child is excessive- there is a standard rule of thumb for time out that is children should only receive one minute for every year in their age, so two year old's would get two minutes, three year old's three minutes, etc.), time outs that place children in extreme isolation such as in a closet, locked in a room, or forced to endure some form of humiliation during the time out such as standing in a corner in front of other children are considered to be particularly harmful.

Positive parenting groups often promote an alternative to the time out; the time in. Time in is creating a safe space for toddlers and other small children to sit and safely re-center themselves. Some parents create a calming space in their home with comfy pillows and blankets, sensorial materials that allow them to feel and touch different textures, and quiet books and even simple craft projects that encourage simple repetitive motions that can be calmly focused on. This allows the parent/caregiver to separate the toddler from the area that is causing them difficulties, but sends a message that the experience is not mean to cause them grief and pain, but rather to allow them the opportunity to get themselves together. The idea behind any discipline we use with our small children should always be to help them create healthy behaviors that will last their entire lives. Time in areas allow them to learn that they can re-center themselves when upset and eventually, this will be a skill they can draw on in any situation and any scenario that they find themselves heated and in need of calming down.

Consistency is Key

In all of these different disciplinary approaches, consistency is key, always. Toddlers will have a hard time learning what is expected of them if not only do disciplinary tactics vary from moment to moment, but from person to person. If the toddler's parents have certain expectations for bedtime and caregivers have a different expectation, then there will always be a certain amount of confusion on what is expected of them in any given situation. This plays back into the importance of routine and how it creates a secure and predictable environment for toddlers when they can know what to expect throughout their day. The same holds true for what to expect in terms of consequences for their actions. If there is a parent that spanks and the other doesn't, then there is now a disconnect in their expectations and their ability to feel safe and secure from day to day. Discipline is about the long game. Unfortunately, it is all too often considered something that parents and caregivers do to force behavior or get children to act the way they want, but that is not it. It is about guiding and teaching toddlers to become the best and healthiest versions of themselves. Parents and caregivers will hopefully remember this as they are setting up their care plans and deciding which methods of guidance will work the best for their toddlers.

Useful Information and Tips for This Chapter

Constructive punishments

For example, when you use a sentence: "You're quite clumsy, look what you did ...", you applied an unconstructive critique. More precisely, you didn't criticize what he did, but him directly (you're clumsy). Constructive criticism would be, "You made a big mess on your desk".

It's the same with praise. When you say, "You're a really wonderful boy, you're mom's angel," you made unconstructive praise. This sentence is encouraging, cheerful, positive for the child, but you didn't praise him for a specific deed. In addition, children who often receive only unconstructive praise - can shut themselves because they realize that the expectations of their environment, and above all their parents, are very high. How will one child dare to make small, childish mistakes if you constantly praise him as smart, grown up, mature, good, obedient ... But when you say, "This is a good drawing you did," or: "You cleaned your room wonderfully, "you sent a clear message to the kid, what pleased you. So always praise or punish, scold or reward a specific action or situation, and not general (dis)satisfaction with the child.

Behavior traffic light

When you determine which of your child's behavior is allowed (green light), which is strictly forbidden (red light) and which deserves the utmost caution because it is on the border of these two (yellow light) and when the child is familiar with these limitations then the need for punishment decreases. Be open enough to keep changing the boundary between prohibited and permitted behaviors, depending on your child's age, but the limit must always exist.

Effects of punishments

To make sure your punishments have an effect, the following is important:

* Talk
Ask your child, "If you were in my place, how would you behave? How would you punish this action?" It is ideal that the same penalties apply to all household members. For example, penalties for not respecting certain agreements, throwing things around the house...

* Do not manipulate with fear of punishment
Explain each punishment to the child. Make a system. When a child knows what punishment is awaiting him for a certain behavior, he himself will have control - whether he will consciously accept

that punishment (not considering his behavior) or not. Therefore, present the penalties in advance.

Never humiliate your child

He has his pride and it's important he keeps it. With humiliation, you may be able to calm both the child and yourself but that will only be on a short term. Do not forget that it is impossible to humiliate the child without leaving any consequences. Also, regardless of the mistake made, never punish him by denying love, the food, by throwing out his favorite toy ... There is simply no child action that could be so bad he would deserve such punishment.

It is very important to "waken" yourself:

Child's actions should not be a trigger for your accumulated feelings to erupt because unfortunately, there are often stress, many obligations and problems, lack of time ... Parental problems of everyday life will certainly affect your mood, but they mustn't be a cause for child punishment. Therefore, when you get angry and begin to yell or differently punish your child, consider whether you are truly angry for something that the child did and deserved punishment or because you have been subjected to unexpressed, suppressed emotions or dissatisfaction (because it is quite possible that you also have your carpet with the mountain below it). Learn self-control! The child does not have to suffer and be punished for your problems, or because you can't direct your aggression to the right source of the problem.

COMMON ISSUES

Parents and caregivers want to do what is best for their children, but if this was easy, there wouldn't be as many books, websites, and parenting theories devoted to helping parents and caregivers work out what's best for their toddlers and their families. There are many areas that are universally tough spots for parents and caregivers and their toddlers, and we will touch on them here.

Parent Perspective

There is an easy fix that has the potential to bring new levels of peace to parents and caregivers, and it requires a simple reframe: In any trying moment when toddler behavior seems to be in immediate need of correction and discipline, before asking how we should do that, first ask why is our toddler doing that? All behavior is communication, and all too often we view toddler behavior through an adult frame of reference. We may watch a toddler that is teasing and taunting their infant sibling mercilessly, and immediately jump to an assumption that they are being naughty and mean to them. If we instead take a moment and really look into the why of the behavior, we may find something more there. For instance, has the toddler been struggling with their new role as older sibling? Has their recently been a new development that made them feel like they were giving something up, perhaps an old beloved baby toy that has now been handed on down to the baby despite their protests to want to keep it for themselves? Does the toddler now find themselves having to fight for their parent's attention? The answers to these questions will shed light on the true why of the behavior, and all parents and caregivers to develop an individualized response that can accurately address the root issue, rather than placing a short-term band-aid type solution.

In this scenario, it sounds like rather than just removing the toddler from access to baby (which is the easy answer here) it will also be important for parents and caregivers to ensure that the toddler feels loved and secure in their place in the family, as a new baby always creates new dynamics that can sometimes make little ones feel displaced.

Always begin with the why before the what to do.

The 'S' Word

The 'S' word is enough to strike confusion into any toddler's heart during a play date: Share!

Unfortunately, parents and caregivers often contribute to the confusion and frustration with the notion of sharing because they often attempt to teach sharing by forcing sharing. It often looks something like this: Toddler one has a toy. Toddler two toddles over and looks longingly at the toy. Toddler two reaches out for the toy. Toddler one pulls the toy back. Toddler two makes a frustrated noise as they reach out for the toy again. Now parent/caregiver of toddler one notices and attempts to teach what they consider to be a valuable lesson and tells toddler one, "share!" while taking the toy out of toddler one's hands and placing it into toddler two's hands. Toddler one erupts into tears.

In this particular scenario, what did the toddlers learn? Toddler one learned that to "share" means that someone will come and take the thing you are using out of your hands and will give it to someone else. Toddler two learned that to "share" means that you want something, so someone else will come and get it for you. Neither toddler understands a bit about what it actually means to share.

To begin with, let's consider what sharing really means. Sharing is the ability to give some of whatever you have to another in a spirit of generosity. Sharing is not having something taken from you or being coerced into giving it. Can you imagine if you were standing at the park in a group of friends when suddenly one of them reaches out for the keys to your car, demanding that you "share"? And then when you react by pulling your car keys away, another friend that is bigger than you pulls them out of your hand and gives them to the other friend, reminding you that it's nice to "share." This would be theft, not sharing!

It is the same thing we do with our small children. Sharing is a developmental skill that comes naturally after they have seen it modeled it before them enough times. Even then, sharing is not always a natural choice for small children to make, and that is developmentally appropriate. It can be very difficult for parents and caregivers to sit back and watch as their toddler pulls back a toy that another toddler wants, but if parents and caregivers can put their own feelings of discomfort aside, they might realize that toddlers are learning important social skills in their song and dance of "I want but can't have" and "I have and won't give." When parents and caregivers step in to 'help,' it takes the opportunity for them to get their bearings and make the required connections away from them.

Sharing is a skill that is learned over time, not forced.

Separation Anxiety

Some toddlers find themselves very anxious when separated from their parents and primary caregivers, but it is often due to how parents and caregivers separate rather than the actual act of separation. There are two extremes that often occur when parents and caregivers are separating from toddlers: On one end of the spectrum, parents and caregivers often try to sneak out and away from their toddler without them realizing it, assuming that if they avoid any tear-filled goodbyes, then there will be no stress and anxiety surrounding their absence. The other end of the spectrum is when parents and caregivers spend too long saying their goodbyes, and return for extra hugs and kisses at the slightest whimper.

The disappearing act is not fooling anybody. It can serve to increase anxiety and agitation in toddlers because not only is their parent/caregiver gone from them, but they are gone without a trace! There is no warning, no explanation, just here one second and gone the next. This is incredibly disrespectful to children and assumes that it is better to leave them hanging in confusion than to deal with their big emotions during goodbyes. There is no need for this.

The long and drawn out goodbye is responsible for making many a toddler wonder, "if my parent can't seem to let me go, then there must really be a reason for it. I must not be safe without them." Toddlers look to their parents and caregivers to be strong, confident leaders. As such, it is necessary for parents and caregivers to project confidence to their toddlers so they know they are safe, they are secure, and they are taken care of. The way to impart this message while leaving is to keep an upbeat, steady voice during the goodbye, and tell your toddler you are leaving now. "Mommy is going to work now, but I love you and will see you very soon! Have fun today." As you are saying this, kisses and hugs can be being exchanged, and then step back and confidently move towards the door. The moment the parent falters and looks back with uncertainty, the toddler recognizes this as a signal that perhaps they are not safe and are not going to be well taken care of. This does an incredible disservice to the toddler.

Calm and Confident Leader

So much of disciplining toddlers in a loving and respectful way depends on this energy, that of a calm and confident leader. Toddlers look to their parents and caregivers for cues on how they should proceed in the world, and modeling is the most effective way to show them what is expected of them.

In all of your interactions with your toddler moving forward, remember this. You can and should respectfully acknowledge their fears, frustrations, issues, and upsets, but you should do this as the calm and confident leader they need. In doing so, you set the tone for both their success, and yours.

ABOUT THE AUTHOR

Nancy Foster, Ph.D. was born in 1963 in Eindhoven, Netherlands, a child psychologist, and a psychotherapist. She is the mother of two outstanding children, now adults with respected careers and their own children. She conveyed her experiences and conclusions that would help them raise their children to become the best possible version of themselves.

She was a professor of developmental psychology at the Radboud University and a longtime associate at a clinic for children with disabilities. She studied academically issues of learning problems, disturbances of instinct and habit in small children, and behavioral disorders of school children.

She spent her whole life fighting for the rights of children and advocated the thesis that there is neither a child nor content that cannot be taught, but a specific situation and a way of acquiring knowledge are responsible for that, emphasized the importance and significance of early development and constructive learning (Bruner's Discovery Learning). She has published several essays and research papers on the challenges of parenting, the problems of families with a hyperactive child, the connection of disorders of learning abilities and learned helplessness, discovery as a source of motivation and others. She developed private practice in the 1990s and deals mainly with counseling of young parents, encouraging psychological and motor development of children and working with children with behavioral disorders of learning abilities. An eclectic approach helps her in the analysis of family dynamics and the child's role in it, and the transformation of maladaptive patterns.

Since 2002 she is the main educator in the parents help center for the parents support with problematic children and the prevention of children's neuroses.

What Did You Think of *Discipline Toddlers in a Loving Way?*

First of all, thank you for purchasing this book **Discipline Toddlers in a Loving Way** I know you could have picked any number of books to read, but you picked this book and for that I am extremely grateful.

I hope that it added at value and quality to your everyday life. If so, it would be really nice if you could share this book with your friends and family by posting to *Facebook* and *Twitter*.

If you enjoyed this book and found some benefit in reading this, I'd like to hear from you and hope that you could take some time to post a review on Amazon. Your feedback and support will help this author to greatly improve his writing craft for future projects and make this book even better. I want you, the reader, to know that your review is very important. I wish you all the best in your future success!

58130750R00068

Made in the USA
Middletown, DE
04 August 2019